A TWISTED TRUTH
UNTANGLED

BY
JOE CREWS

1. What and Where Is Hell? 2
2. Punishment After the Judgment 5
3. No Second Death
      Before the Resurrection 10
4. Location of Hell 12
5. Hell-Fire Not Endless 14
6. Unquenchable Fire 18
7. Body and Soul Destroyed 25
8. God's Justice Vindicated 27
9. No More Pain of Death 29
10. Hell Not Intended for Us 31

CHAPTER ONE
WHAT AND WHERE IS HELL?

One of the most theologically confused subjects in the Bible is that of hell. It has been fumbled by the clergy and distorted by the laity until the word has become best known as a common vulgarism and expletive. Everywhere people are asking the same questions: What and where is hell? What is the fate of the wicked? Will a God of love torture people throughout eternity? Will the fire of hell ever burn the wickedness out of sinners?

These questions deserve sound Bible answers. The controversy surrounding the subject should not discourage us from exposing all the truth as it is in Christ. First, we need to understand that there is a heaven to win and a hell to shun. Jesus taught that every soul would be either saved or lost. There is no neutral place, and there are no second prizes. "The Son of man shall send forth his angels, and they shall gather out of his kingdom all things that offend, And them which do iniquity; and shall cast them into a furnace of fire: there shall be wailing and gnashing of teeth. Then shall the righteous shine forth as the sun in the kingdom of their Father" (Matthew 13:41–43).

In view of these two ultimate destinies for all who have ever been born, how earnest we should be in seeking to find the right way. Christ said, "I am the way, the truth and the life." The only absolute safety for anyone is to take exactly what Jesus taught about hell. His doctrine is the only one that is wholly dependable and true. He said some will be cast into the fire, and some will shine forth in the kingdom.

Strangely enough, Christ has been charged by many religious leaders with teaching a falsehood on this subject. They have accused Him of teaching that an immortal soul flies away from the body at death to either heaven or hell. This is not what Jesus taught at all. He never gave the least intimation that some disembodied soul separates from the body at the time of death. Surely, He did not ever give the impression that the wicked suffer an eternal torment as soon as they die.

Now let's get a sample of what Jesus really taught on the subject of hell. "And if thy hand offend thee, cut it off: it is better for thee to enter into life maimed, than having two hands to go into hell …" (Mark 9:43). These words of the Master prove beyond any shadow of doubt that it is the body that goes into the fire, and not some mystical soul. In Matthew 5:30 He spoke of the "whole body" being cast into hell. That means hands, feet, eyes, and all the other members of the physical body.

In contrast to the doctrine of Christ, modern pulpits resound with dramatic portrayals of imaginary souls leaving the body at death—souls that have neither substance nor shape. This view, popular though it may be, is totally contrary to what Jesus taught. Mark it well, for the great Master Teacher spelled it out repeatedly in the gospels—those who are cast into the fire of hell will go there with hands, feet, eyes, and all the physical features of the body. They will not go in some ethereal state of formless spirit or soul.

Now we are prepared to examine four great facts from the Bible that will illuminate most of the questions that have been asked about the fate of the wicked.

CHAPTER TWO
PUNISHMENT AFTER THE JUDGMENT

The first important fact about hell is this: *The unsaved do not go to any place of punishment as soon as they die, but are reserved in the grave until the day of judgment to be punished.* Christ explicitly taught this truth in the well-known parable of the wheat and the tares. After the householder had sown the wheat in the field, his servant came to report that tares were growing among the grain. His question was whether he should pull up the weeds while they were still very small. The householder's answer was, "Nay; lest while ye gather up the tares, ye root up also the wheat with them. Let both grow together until the harvest: and in the time of the harvest I will say to the reapers, Gather ye together first the tares, and bind them in bundles to burn them; but gather the wheat into my barn" (Matthew 13:29, 30).

Now follow the words of Christ as He explains the meaning of the parable: "He that soweth the good seed is the Son of man; The field is the world; the good seed are the children of the kingdom; but the tares are the children of the wicked one; The enemy that sowed them is the devil; the harvest is the end of the world; and the reapers are the angels. As therefore the tares are gathered and burned in the fire; so shall it be in the end of this world. The Son of man shall send forth his angels, and they shall gather out of his kingdom all things that offend, and them which do iniquity; And shall cast them into a furnace of fire: there shall be wailing and gnashing of teeth" (Matthew 13:37–43).

No one can simplify the parable by enlarging on what Jesus said. It is so clear that a child can understand it. He said the tares represented the wicked people, and that they would be cast into the fire "at the end of the world." It was in the harvest that the separation would take place, and He plainly stated, "The harvest is the end of the world." How can anyone misconstrue these words of Christ? The whole idea of the wicked going into the fire at the time of death contradicts our Lord's specific teaching that they would be cast into the fire at the end of the world.

Since the judgment also takes place after Christ comes, we can see how impossible it would be for anyone to be punished before that time. Justice demands that a person be brought into judgment before being punished. Peter declared, "The Lord knoweth how to deliver the godly out of temptations, and to reserve the unjust unto the day of judgment to be punished" (2 Peter 2:9). That certainly makes sense, doesn't it? Suppose a man should be brought into the court accused of stealing, and the judge said, "Put him away for ten years; then we'll try his case." Listen, even a human judge would not be that unfair! He would be impeached for such an action. Surely, God would not be guilty of such a farce.

If we let the Bible mean what it says, there can be no doubt on this point. The wicked are "reserved" until when? Until the "day of judgment." To be what? "To be punished"! This means they cannot be punished before that judgment day. Does the Bible tell where they are reserved until then? Christ Himself said, "Marvel not at this: for the hour is coming, in which all that are in the graves shall hear his voice, and shall come forth; they that have done good, unto the resurrection of life; and they that have done evil, unto the resurrection of damnation" (John 5:28, 29).

How plain! Jesus said that both good and bad would come forth *from their graves* to receive either life or damnation. This proves that from the time of death until they come forth in the resurrection they are not receiving any recompense or punishment. It all happens after they come forth. They are reserved until that day just as Peter indicated, but Christ spelled out where they will be reserved—"in the graves."

If plainer words are needed, listen to Jesus speaking in Luke 14:14, "Thou shalt be recompensed at the resurrection of the just." Or hear Him again in Matthew 16:27, "For the Son of man shall come in the glory of his Father with his angels; and then he shall reward every man according to his works." When is "then"? When He comes with His angels. No reward or recompense is handed out until the resurrection of the just, when He comes with all the angels. These verses are beyond controversy. Taken in their context, they contain no ambiguity or hidden meaning.

Again Christ is quoted in the very last chapter of the Bible, "And, behold, I come quickly; and my reward is with me, to give every man according as his work shall be" (Revelation 22:12). Here He reminds us that "every man"—every person—will receive his just reward when Christ returns to this earth. Job declares, "that the wicked is reserved to the day of destruction. They shall be brought forth to the day of wrath." Daniel wrote that they which "sleep in the dust of the earth shall awake, some to everlasting life, and some to shame and everlasting contempt" (Daniel 12:2).

Can there be any doubt where the wicked are reserved before facing resurrection, judgment, and punishment? We have the testimony of Peter, Daniel, Job and the Master Himself. There is no room to quibble. They are reserved in the grave.

Now we come to the second great fact about hell: *None of the unsaved will be cast into hell-fire until after the second coming of Jesus at the end of the world.* Although we have already seen substantial evidence on this point, let's look even more. Describing the punishment of the wicked, John wrote: "But the fearful, and unbelieving, and the abominable, and murderers, and whoremongers, and sorcerers, and idolaters and all liars, shall have their part in the lake which burneth with fire and brimstone: which is the second death" (Revelation 21:8).

CHAPTER THREE
NO SECOND DEATH BEFORE THE RESURRECTION

Here the lost are pictured in the fires of hell, suffering the punishment for their sins. And what is that punishment? "The second death," says John. Do you realize what this proves about the wicked? It proves they will not be cast into the lake of fire until after the resurrection takes place. These people die the second death in the fire, but they cannot suffer a second death until they get a second life. They lived the first life in this world and died the first death, going into the grave. Before they can die a second death they must be resurrected—they must be given a second life. This, of course, is what happens at the end of the world. Jesus said, "All that are in the graves shall come forth."

Now after getting that second life in the resurrection, the wicked will be punished for their sins in hell-fire, "which is the second death." By the way, that second death is the final, eternal death from which there will be no resurrection. But the point to be noted is the *time of this hell-fire punishment*—it is after the resurrection at the end of the world. It does not take place at the time of the first death as so many have been led to believe.

Does the Bible tell us how the wicked will be cast into the lake of fire? Yes, it does. John describes the dramatic events that take place at the close of the millennium. "And when the thousand years are expired, Satan shall be loosed out of his prison, And shall go out to deceive the nations which are in the four quarters of the earth, Gog and Magog, to gather them together to battle: the number of whom is as the sand of the sea. And they went up on the breadth of the earth, and compassed the camp of the saints about, and the beloved city: and fire came down from God out of heaven, and devoured them" (Revelation 20:7–9).

Here at the end of the millennium all the wicked people who have ever lived will come forth in the second resurrection. After describing how the righteous would come to life and reign with Christ during the thousand years, John wrote, "But the rest of the dead lived not again until the thousand years were finished" (Revelation 20:5).

The rest of the dead, of course, had to be the wicked, and their resurrection will provide opportunity for Satan to take up his continuing battle against God and the saints. He goes out to gather the host of lost ones, who have been raised from the dead. He has people to deceive once more, and he convinces them that they can prevail against the New Jerusalem that has descended from God out of heaven (Revelation 21:2). As they march up and encompass the city, the wicked are suddenly cut down by the devouring fire that rains upon them from heaven. *This is the hell-fire that is the final punishment for sin.*

CHAPTER FOUR
LOCATION OF HELL

The Bible clearly asserts that this fire devours the wicked right here on "the breadth of the earth." Every Bible writer who speaks on the subject of hell adds new insight on this second death of the wicked. Peter states: "But the heavens and the earth, which are now, by the same word are kept in store, reserved unto fire against the day of judgment and perdition of ungodly men" (2 Peter 3:7). Then he goes on to describe the day of the Lord that will melt the very elements with fervent heat.

The language of Peter is very explicit about the place of punishment for the ungodly. He says this earth is reserved for that fire which will bring judgment and perdition to the wicked. Their punishment will be in this earth. Isaiah declared, "For it is the day of the LORD's vengeance, and the year of recompenses for the controversy of Zion. And the streams thereof shall be turned into brimstone, and the land thereof shall become burning pitch" (Isaiah 34:8, 9).

The prophet portrays the entire planet enveloped in the destroying fire. Even the streams and dust are transformed into an exploding combustion of pitch and brimstone. Isaiah says this is God's vengeance and "recompense" at the end of the controversy.

David adds to the testimony with these words, "Upon the wicked he shall rain snares, fire, and brimstone, and an horrible tempest: this shall be the portion of their cup" (Psalm 11:6). Notice that he uses almost the same words as John and Peter in describing the fate of the wicked. All agree as to the place of the punishment (the earth) and the agent of punishment (fire).

This brings us to the third great fact about the subject of hell: *Hell as a place of punishment will be this earth turned into a lake of fire at the Day of Judgment.* However, this also raises some other very interesting questions about the fate of the lost. One of the most intriguing and puzzling has to do with the length of punishment. How long will the wicked continue to live and suffer in that fire?

No one can answer that question precisely because the Bible says they will be punished according to their works. This means there will be degrees of punishment. Some will suffer longer than others will. But one thing we can say with certainty—the wicked won't live in that fire throughout eternity.

CHAPTER FIVE
HELL-FIRE NOT ENDLESS

There are several reasons for being so sure on this point. First, this earth is also declared the final home for the righteous. Jesus said, "Blessed are the meek: For they shall inherit the earth" (Matthew 5:5). Peter, after describing this earth exploding and burning with a great noise, saw a new earth filled with righteousness. "Nevertheless we, according to his promise, look for new heavens and a new earth, wherein dwelleth righteousness" (2 Peter 3:13).

The wicked cannot continue to live in this planet because it has been specifically promised, in its entirety, to Abraham's spiritual seed (Romans 4:13). After being purged of all the curse of sin, it will revert to the first dominion and to God's original plan for it. It will be finally what God intended it to be—a perfect home for a perfect people.

In the second place, the wicked cannot continue to live in this earth because they have never trusted Christ for eternal life. It is only the righteous who receive the gift of eternal life. "For God so loved the world, that he gave his only begotten Son that whosoever believeth in him should not perish. ..." (John 3:16). But what about those who don't believe in him? They surely will perish. The Bible says, "The wages of sin is death" (Romans 6:23).

Please don't miss the pointed simplicity of these verses. The wicked are never promised life. They are promised death—eternal death. Only the righteous are promised life—eternal life.

But there is only one way to get life without end, and that is through faith in Jesus. John describes it this way: "And this is the record, that God hath given to us eternal life, and this life is in his Son. He that hath the Son hath life; and he that hath not the Son of God hath not life" (1 John 5:11, 12). Let me ask you a question: Do those wicked ones in the lake of fire have the Son of God? Of course not. Then how could they have life? John says, "Ye know that no murderer hath eternal life abiding in him" (1 John 3:15). Will those murderers in hell-fire continue to have life for eternity? Never.

It would be the rankest heresy to believe that eternal life could be obtained from some other source than Jesus. Where would the wicked get it? Paul declares that Jesus Christ "hath brought life and immortality to light *through the gospel*" (2 Timothy 1:10). Inspiration reveals no other source of immortality except through the gospel of Christ. Where is a text in the Bible that describes the conferring of immortality upon the wicked? You can read often about the righteous receiving it, but never the unbeliever.

Paul said, "Behold I shew you a mystery; We shall not all sleep, but we shall all be changed, In a moment, in the twinkling of an eye, at the last trump: for the trumpet shall sound, and the dead shall be raised incorruptible, and we shall be changed. For this corruptible must put on incorruption, and this mortal must put on immortality" (1 Corinthians 15:51–53).

This text speaks of a certain point in time when the righteous will be instantly changed into immortal beings. That time is still future. It occurs when Jesus returns, at the last trumpet sound, when the resurrection takes place. Nowhere in the Bible do we read of the wicked being changed in this manner. And it is precisely because they never receive this gift of eternal life that they are unable to keep living in the lake of fire.

It is inconceivable and unreasonable to fabricate such an event. It is contrary to the Bible and repugnant to the senses. Ezekiel declared, "The soul that sinneth, it shall die"

(Ezekiel 18:4). No matter what we understand a soul to be, let's accept the simple Bible fact that it can die and will die because of sin.

If the wicked live eternally in the fire, then they have the same thing as the righteous except in a different place. Who could give them eternal life but Christ? John 3:16 settles this issue so clearly and simply. Those who do not believe in the only begotten Son will *perish.* They will die. They will die the second death—an eternal death from which they will never be raised. That death will never end. It is an endless, eternal punishment, because it is an endless, eternal death.

CHAPTER SIX
UNQUENCHABLE FIRE

Someone may raise this question: What about the unquenchable fire that burns the wicked? Doesn't that mean it will never go out? Of course, it doesn't. To quench means to extinguish or put out. No one will be able to put out the fire of hell. That is the strange fire of God. No one will be able to escape from it by extinguishing it.

Isaiah says of that fire, "Behold, they shall be as stubble; the fire shall burn them; they shall not deliver themselves from the power of the flame: there shall not be a coal to warm at, nor a fire to sit before it" (Isaiah 47:14). After it has accomplished its work of destruction, that fire will go out. No one can deliver themselves from its flame by putting it out, but finally not a coal will be left. So say the Scriptures.

Jeremiah prophesied that Jerusalem would burn with a fire that could not be quenched (Jeremiah 17:27), but it burned down to ashes (2 Chronicles 36:19–21). Read those verses and see how the Bible uses the word "quench." It does not mean fire that will never go out. It only means what it says, "unquenchable." It cannot be quenched.

And what can we say about the expressions "eternal" and "everlasting" which are used to describe the fires of hell? There is absolutely no confusion or contradiction when we allow the Bible to supply its own definition of terms. Many make the mistake of applying modern definitions to those biblical words without reference to their ancient contextual usage. This violates one of the most fundamental rules of interpretation.

The fact is that eternal fire does not mean a fire that will never go out. The same expression is used in Jude 7 concerning the destruction of Sodom and Gomorrha. "Even as Sodom and Gomorrha, and the cities about them in like manner, giving themselves over to fornication, and going after strange flesh, are set forth as an example, suffering the vengeance of eternal fire."

It is obvious that Sodom is not still burning today. The Dead Sea rolls over the place where those ancient cities once stood. Yet, they burned with "eternal fire," and we are told that it was an example of something. Of what is it an example? "And turning the cities of Sodom and Gomorrha into ashes condemned them with an overthrow, making them an ensample unto those that after should live ungodly" (2 Peter 2:6).

There it is! That eternal fire which brought Sodom to ashes is an example of what will finally happen to the wicked. If this text is true, the same kind of fire that destroyed Sodom and Gomorrha will also burn the wicked in the lake of fire. It will have to be eternal fire. Does that mean it will also burn the wicked to ashes? The Bible says yes. "For behold, the day cometh that shall burn as an oven; and all the proud, yea, and all that do wickedly, shall be stubble: and the day that cometh shall burn them up, saith the LORD of hosts, that it shall leave them neither root nor branch … And ye shall tread down the wicked; for they shall be ashes under the soles of your feet in the day that I shall do this, saith the LORD of hosts" (Malachi 4:1, 3).

No words of any language could make it more forceful or clear. This eternal fire burns up eternally. Even Satan, the root, is finally consumed. How consistent the whole picture appears as we let the Bible explain its own terms. What devious manipulation of words would be required to evade the obvious meaning of these words? Yet those who have been prejudiced by a lifetime of tradition can read those words "burn them up … they shall be ashes" and still insist that the wicked are alive and suffering.

Admittedly, there are some ambiguous verses on this subject, but we are finding that they all harmonize when the context is considered, and the Bible is allowed to be its own commentary.

Even Christ's words in Matthew 25:46 are not confusing when we take the obvious meaning. "And these shall go away into everlasting punishment: but the righteous into life eternal." Many are troubled over the expression, "everlasting punishment," but notice that it does not say "everlasting punishing." Whatever the punishment is, it will last eternally. Does the Bible tell us what the punishment is? Of course. "The wages of sin is death" (Romans 6:23). Therefore, Jesus was simply saying that the death would be everlasting. It would never end. It would never be broken by a resurrection.

Paul simplifies it further with these words: "In flaming fire taking vengeance on them that know not God, and that obey not the gospel of our Lord Jesus Christ: Who shall be punished?" Now, listen, Paul is going to tell us what the punishment is. "Who shall be punished with everlasting destruction from the presence of the Lord, and from the glory of his power" (2 Thessalonians 1:8, 9). Therefore, the punishment is everlasting destruction—a destruction that is everlasting. From it, there will be no resurrection or hope of life.

But what about that worm which dieth not? Many have read the words of Jesus about hell, "Where their worm dieth not and the fire is not quenched" (Mark 9:45, 46). Some have interpreted the worm to be the soul. Is that what Jesus meant? Nowhere in the Bible is there any allusion to the soul as a worm.

In this instance, Jesus used the word "Gehenna" for the word "hell." It so happened that Gehenna was an actual place of burning just outside the walls of Jerusalem. No doubt, Christ's listeners could see the smoke curling up from the Valley of Gehenna, where dead bodies and garbage were constantly being burned. If anything fell outside the destructive flames, maggots or worms quickly consumed it. With the vivid scenes of utter extinction before their eyes, Jesus used the Gehenna fire as an example of the complete destruction of hell-fire. The fire was never quenched, and the worms were constantly at work upon the bodies—a picture of total destruction.

Perhaps the most easily misconstrued text about hell is John's allusion to the smoke ascending "for ever and ever." For those who are unfamiliar with other uses of this phrase in the Bible, it can be very confusing indeed. But a comparison of verses in both Old and New

Testaments reveal that the words "for ever" are used 57 times in the Bible in reference to something that has already ended. In other words, "for ever" does not always mean "without end."

Many notable examples could be cited, but two or three are noteworthy. In Exodus 21, the conditions are laid down concerning the law of servitude. If a servant chose to continue serving the master he loved rather than his freedom when it came due, then his ear was to be pierced with an awl and the Scripture declares, "He shall serve him for ever" (verse 6). But how long would that servant serve his human master? Only as long as he lived, of course. So, the words "for ever" did not mean without end.

Hannah took her son Samuel to God's temple, where he would "there abide for ever" (1 Samuel 1:22). Yet in verse 28 we are plainly told, "As long as he liveth he shall be lent to the Lord." The original meaning of the term "for ever" indicates an indefinite period of time. Generally, it defines the period of time in which something can continue to exist under the circumstances prevailing. Even Jonah's stay in the whale's belly is described by him as "for ever" (Jonah 2:6).

Someone may object that this could also limit the life of the righteous in heaven, because they are described as glorifying God forever. The terms are the same for both the saved and the lost. But there is one tremendous difference in the circumstances involved. The saints have received the gift of immortality. Their life now measures with the life of God. Immortality means "not subject to death." The words "for ever" used in reference to them could only mean "without end," because they are immortal subjects already. But when "for ever" is used to describe the wicked, we are talking about mortal creatures who can die and must die. Their "for ever" is only as long as their mortal nature can survive in the fire which punishes them according to their works.

CHAPTER SEVEN
SOUL AND BODY DESTROYED

This brings us to the final fact concerning the fate of the wicked: *After the unsaved are punished according to their sins, they will be wiped out of existence, both body and soul.* Jesus states it very simply, "And fear not them which kill the body but rather fear him which is able to destroy both soul and body in hell" (Matthew 10:28).

In the light of this statement, how can anyone continue to claim immortality for the wicked? Jesus, the only One who can bestow the gift of life, rejects the possibility that those in hell can continue to live in any form whatsoever. The life will be snuffed out for eternity, and the body will be annihilated in the flames.

The psalmist wrote: "But the wicked shall perish, and the enemies of the LORD shall be as the fat of lambs: they shall consume; into smoke shall they consume away" (Psalm 37:20). "For yet a little while, and the wicked shall not be: yea, thou shalt diligently consider his place, and it shall not be" (verse 10).

The most powerful, definitive words in human language are used to describe the destruction in hell, but people still insist that the writers do not really mean what their words express. "Destroy," "consume," "burn" "devour," "death"—do these words have some mysterious, opposite meaning in the Bible than they have in other books? We have no reason to think so. The fact is that theology has made an ogre out of our great God of love. He has been portrayed as crueler than Hitler. Even though Hitler tortured people and experimented with them, finally he allowed them to die. But God will keep these deathless souls alive for the purpose of seeing them writhe and scream throughout eternity, so the theologians claim.

CHAPTER EIGHT
God's Justice Vindicated

Not only is such a picture misrepresentative of God's love, it also distorts His justice. Think for a moment about the implications of a doctrine that would consign every lost soul to an immediate, never-ending hell at the time of death. Suppose a man died 5,000 years ago with one cherished sin in his life. His soul would go instantly into the fire to be tormented for eternity. Then picture another death; that of Adolph Hitler, who supervised the deaths of millions of people. According to the popular doctrine, his soul also would immediately enter hell to suffer eternally. But the man, who was lost because of only one sin, will burn 5,000 years longer than Hitler will. How could that be just? Would God deal in such a manner? It would contradict the Bible statement that each one must be punished according to his works.

There are two extreme views in current circulation concerning the punishment of the wicked. One is Universalism, which contends that God is too good to allow anyone to be lost. The other is the awful doctrine of endless torment that would perpetuate for all eternity a dark abyss of anguish and suffering. Both are wrong. The truth lies in between. God will punish the wicked according to their works, but He will not immortalize evil in the process.

I truly believe that many honest souls have been turned away from God because of their revulsion at this misrepresentation of His character. They can't love someone who would arbitrarily keep evil people in endless torment with no purpose in view. No rehabilitation is possible. Only a vindictive spirit of revenge could be served by such an unspeakable arrangement. Is God like that?

After hearing the Bible truth about hell, a bank president threw his arms around my shoulders and said, "Joe, I'm a believer again. For years I've been an agnostic because I had been taught that God would torture the wicked eternally."

CHAPTER NINE
NO MORE PAIN OR DEATH

Someday soon, God will have a clean universe. All the effects of sin will be banished forever. There will be no sin, no sinners and no devil to tempt. It will be exactly as God planned it in the beginning.

John described that future home in these words, "And God shall wipe away all tears from their eyes; and there shall be no more death, neither sorrow, nor crying, neither shall there be any more pain: for the former things are passed away" (Revelation 21:4).

Can you find any room in those precious words for any suffering on the part of anybody in the whole recreated universe? God said crying and pain would be no more. Do you believe His Word or do you choose to believe man's surmising? Just four verses before writing this promise, John described how the wicked would be cast into the lake of fire. "And whosoever was not found written in the book of life was cast into the lake of fire. And I saw a new heaven and a new earth: for the first heaven and the first earth were passed away" (Revelation 20:15; 21:1).

That lake of fire is right here on planet earth according to Revelation 20:9. But please notice that this place where the wicked burn will pass away and God will re-create the *new* earth in its stead. The New Jerusalem descends before that fire devours the wicked, and afterwards, according to verse 4, there will be no more sorrow, pain, crying, or death.

In order for no more pain to exist, there can be no eternal hell existing either. The two things are mutually exclusive of each other. We should thank God every day that His plan will finally end suffering. Satan will not be here to cause pain, and God promises that His new kingdom will not even contain a shadow of a pain.

CHAPTER TEN
HELL NOT INTENDED FOR US

Finally, we should rejoice that hell was never intended for you and me. Jesus said it was "prepared for the devil and his angels." (Matthew 25:41). If we stumble into that fire, it will be the most colossal blunder we could ever make. You would have to go there over the broken body of Jesus Christ and in spite of the Father's love, the Holy Spirit's pleading, and the heavenly influence of a million angels. The most unanswerable question in the whole world is this: "How shall we escape if we neglect so great a salvation?" There is no answer because there is no escape except through Christ and His cross.

No one will be lost because he sinned, because everyone has sinned. No one will be left out of heaven because he lied, stole, or committed adultery. The only reason anyone will be lost is that he refuses to turn away from his sin into the arms of a loving Saviour who stands ready to pardon and cleanse from all unrighteousness. "For God so loved the world that he gave his only begotten Son, that whosoever believeth in him should not perish, but have everlasting life" (John 3:16).